WRITING FOR KIDS

WRITING FOR KIDS

Carol Lea Benjamin

THOMAS Y. CROWELL   NEW YORK

Library of Congress Cataloging in Publication Data
Benjamin , Carol Lea.
   Writing for kids.

   Summary: An introduction to writing discussing such
aspects as how to get ideas as well as how to work from
sentence to paragraph to finished story or essay.
   1. English language—Composition and exercises—
Juvenile literature.   [1. English language—Composition
and exercises]   I. Title.
PE1408.B475 1985   808′.042′0880544   85-47542
ISBN 0-690-04490-9 (lib. bdg.)

   "Harper trophy books."
ISBN 0-06-446012-6 (pbk.)   85-42831

For Bruce Harold Wolk

It is not often that someone comes along
who is a true friend and a good writer.

E. B. WHITE, *Charlotte's Web*

Contents

1. Meet the Author—It's You!   1
2. Writing for Kids   7
3. "What If I Can't Think of Anything to Write?"   14
4. Illustrated Sentences   17
5. Creating Books   24
6. A Writer's Notebook   33
7. Ah! Inspiration!   35
8. What I Did On My Summer Vacation   69
9. Wonderful Words   73
10. Sentence to Paragraph to Finished Piece   78
11. Private Writing: Keeping a Journal   87
12. Professional Secrets You Can Use   94
13. Meet the Author—It's Me!   98
    Index   101

ACKNOWLEDGMENTS

The author wishes to thank the following writers whose works appear in this book:

E. B. White, William Cowper, Tina Mummery, Maria Beatty, Jay Rubinstein, Judy Blume, Gerald Durrell, Kathy Weinert, Joy Adamson, Michele Bean, Roger Tory Peterson, Celia Converse, William Zinsser, Isaac Bashevis Singer, Peter DeVries, Victor Hugo, Anais Nin, Rebecca Lobl, Will Rogers, Russell Baker, Lynn Offerman, Washington Irving, Paul Zindel, M. E. Kerr, James Joyce, George Orwell, Jack Finney, Bram Stoker, Michael Krieg, Gustave Flaubert, Andy Weiss, Richard Adams, Woody Allen, Robbie Dewey, Betsy Ehrenfeld, Saul Bellow, Bruce Harold Wolk, Ann Seranne, Yogi Berra, Sarah Thomas, Hester Mundis, Diane Arbus, William Shakespeare, Lewis Carroll, Mark Twain, Leonard Baskin, Martin Cruz Smith, Isak Dinesen, William Steig, James Thurber, Lewis Thomas, Frank Conroy, Leo Tolstoy, Henry Roth, J. D. Salinger, Norman Mailer, Harry Mazer, Robertson Davies, Jean de Brunhoff, J.R.R. Tolkien, E. M. Forster, George Bernard Shaw, T. J. Siegal, Anne Frank, Robert Browning, and my kids, Victoria Halboth and Jennifer Lennard.

Warm thanks, too, to Orson Bean, founder of The Fifteenth Street School, where I once taught and where much of the material by children was written.

And a written reminder of my appreciation and affection for some good people—
    my agent, Willam Reiss
    my editor, Marilyn Kriney
    my friend, Mordecai Siegal
    my sweetheart, Stephen Lennard
    and absent friend, Mary Ann Gillies—still thinking of you.

For a list of sources of the quotations that appear in this book, see page 100.

WRITING FOR KIDS

1

Meet the Author— It's You!

Know thyself.

INSCRIPTION AT THE DELPHIC ORACLE

NOTE WELL: IF THIS IS A LIBRARY BOOK, PLEASE DO NOT WRITE IN IT. INSTEAD, COPY "MEET THE AUTHOR" ONTO SOME LOOSE-LEAF PAPER, WHICH YOU CAN EVENTUALLY ADD TO YOUR WRITER'S NOTEBOOK.

My name is _____, but sometimes I'd like to change it to _____. Here are some things I like about me: _____
_____ .

And here are some things I don't like: _____
_____ .

1

If I were President of the United States, here are three things I'd do:

_____

_____

_____.

I was born in _____ and now I live in _____. Someday I'd like to visit the following places: _____

_____

My best friends are _____

_____.

These are the qualities I like in a friend: _____

_____.

My favorite foods are: _____

_____ . The food I hate most is

_____.

My favorite animal is a _____. This is a picture of it.

My favorite game is _____. Here are the rules
for playing it: _____

_____

_____

_____

_____.

My favorite book is _____ by

_____. It is about _____

_____

_____.

These are three things that make me mad!

_____

_____

_____

These are three things that make me sad.

_____

_____

_____

These are three things that make me glad!

_____

_____

_____

3

Here are the words of my favorite song:

_____

_____

_____

_____ .

When I am alone, I like to _____ .

My nastiest thought is _____

_____

_____ .

My sweetest wish is _____

_____ .

NOTE: FOR THESE PAGES, USE PHOTOGRAPHS OR MAKE DRAWINGS.

This is my mother.

This is my father.

Here's what I looked like when I was born.

Here's what I look like now.

Writing for Kids

Variety's the very spice of life.

WILLIAM COWPER

From our earliest ancestors' first scratchings on the garden wall—

> Adam,
> We ran out of fruit. Back soon.
> Eve

to the poem of a modern kid—

Ice Cream

I think in the wintertime
Of cones of ice cream—
Chocolate, cherry, blueberry and lime.
In the spring they are not a dream.

TINA MUMMERY (10)

writing has always helped people to communicate.

Sometimes writing things down satisfies the urgent need to communicate with yourself. Writing can help you remember significant events in your life:

Janis

When we got a new cat that is called Janis, we thought that she was fat. And my father is a doctor. And I said that Janis is pregnant. And my father said that isn't true. And Janis started getting even fatter. So we took Janis to the vet. And the vet said that she is pregnant. And my father said, "Oh, no!" And one week later Janis had four kittens. And now she's going to have some more kittens.

MARIA BEATTY (9)

It can help you clarify thoughts and sort out feelings:

Growing Up

Growing up sometimes is terrible
But sometimes it's fun.
It pushes, oh, it pushes
Like the pin in a gun.
All the bad things around you
All the responsibilities to take—

Sometimes I feel
Like I really might break.
But there are fun things about it
Like the sun and the snow—
That's one reason why
I do want to grow.

JAY RUBINSTEIN (10)

Writing can express love, sadness, fear, or anger in a safe arena:

Are you there God? It's me, Margaret. We're moving today. I'm so scared God. I've never lived anywhere but here. Suppose I hate my new school? Suppose everybody there hates me? Please help me God. Don't let New Jersey be too horrible. Thank you.

JUDY BLUME, *Are You There God? It's Me, Margaret.*

It can record ideas and plans:

"What we all need," said Larry, getting into his stride again, "is sunshine…a country where we can *grow*."

"Yes, dear, that would be nice," agreed Mother, not really listening.

9

"I had a letter from George this morning—he says Corfu's wonderful. Why don't we pack up and go to Greece?"

"Very well, dear, if you like," said Mother unguardedly.

GERALD DURRELL, My Family and Other Animals

or preserve your impressions:

Daddy picked me up on his shoulders and rode me to the stairs. My mother had gone to get me milk with a vitamin pill. My flannels were itchy. The milk was warm and the pill tasted funny. At first it wouldn't go down. The bubbles of milk stuck to the insides of the glass. The bubbles of milk—the milk that was warm—

CAROL KAHN, "I Am a Little Girl" (17)

Writing can be a playground for your imagination, a place in which you fool around with words and ideas, just for your own pleasure:

Once I shota
Pink and purple polka dota
Hippopota

It hurts, it hurts
Cried Hippopota
Revenge shall come
From Mudda—Fadda

KATHY WEINERT (11)

Writing is also an effective way to communicate with others. It can be a way to express emotion:

The river flowed slowly in front of us, as it had flowed yesterday and it would flow tomorrow. A hornbill called, some dry leaves fell off the tree and were carried away by the water. Elsa was part of this life. She belonged to nature and not to man. We were "man" and we loved her and she had been brought up to love us. Would she be able to forget all that had been familiar to her until this morning? Would she go and hunt when she was hungry? Or would she wait trustfully for our return, knowing that up to now we had never let her down?

JOY ADAMSON, *Born Free: A Lioness of Two Worlds*

Writing can be something you do in school, to be read, commented on, and graded by your teacher:

Pine Tree

The pine tree way up high
Sways to the wind
As the branches swing
The pine cones are scattered
Around the dirt.

MICHELE BEAN (11)

Or writing can be a method of transmitting information:

Few men have souls so dead that they will not bother to look up when they hear the barking of wild Geese. For Geese symbolize the mystery of migration more than any other birds, and as harbingers of spring, they are second only to the Robin.

ROGER TORY PETERSON, *How to Know the Birds*

It can be a piece of reporting for the school newspaper, a play to be performed in school or with your family, or a funny poem, written just to make your friends laugh:

Fred

Fred was a bear
To keep him warm
He has lots of hair
So when winter comes
He won't need thermal underwear.

CELIA CONVERSE (10)

Whether you plan to share your writing with others or keep it to yourself, first of all, it should please you. The most important audience for any writer is himself:

> You are writing primarily to entertain yourself, and if you go about it with confidence you will also entertain the readers who are worth writing for. If you lose the dullards back in the dust, that's where they belong.

WILLIAM ZINSSER, On Writing Well

Anyone can learn to write. Any person of any age can discover how to enjoy the process of writing, the putting together of words, phrases, sentences, and paragraphs.

Helping you to enjoy—and improve at—both public and private writing is the goal of this book.

"What If I Can't Think of Anything to Write?"

The wastebasket is a writer's best friend.

ISAAC BASHEVIS SINGER

To some people, the sight of a blank sheet of paper is enough to cause panic. They get scared and freeze up. Their minds go as blank as the piece of paper. Having to write on demand can make them feel small, sweaty, sick, or stupid.

Yet every person, child or adult, has a world of experience to call upon and write about. Everyone has wishes and dreams, fantasies and ideas. Everyone is full of stories— things that really happened, things they can make up. Still, when you feel pressured and afraid, it is difficult to get in touch with your own material.

If you have ever felt scared and unable to write when you had to, here's an experiment to try at home. Sit down at a desk or table with a piece of paper in front of you. Take a deep breath, then exhale. Now, with both hands, carefully pick up the piece of paper and...CRUNCH IT UP INTO A BALL. And now slam dunk it into the wastebasket.

Perhaps you are thinking, "I just wasted a tree!"

If you are going to write well, you are going to use up a lot of trees.

Even so, you can retrieve that piece of paper from the wastebasket, smooth it out, and write on it. Perhaps you have worried about making inkblots or smudges on your clean piece of paper. Perhaps you are so worried about being neat that you can't write a good story. So, be a slob.

Let your ballpoint leak.

Smudge away.

Make some dirty fingerprints.

Rip off a corner of the page.

Write your name in the middle of the page—and much too large. (You can even misspell it!)

Now add a funny picture.

Then tear up the page and throw it away.

That piece of paper was well used. It showed you you're the boss.

It's one thing to feel relaxed around the tools of your trade—leaky ballpoints, paper, dictionaries, pencils, and erasers. But what if you still can't think of anything to write?

Start small. Start with a sentence.

A single sentence can be so colorful, so funny, so true, so rich in atmosphere or packed with emotion, that it gets caught in your mind the way burrs get stuck to a woolly dog. The next chapter will focus on single sentences and some surprising things you can do with them.

Illustrated Sentences

One picture is worth more than ten thousand words.

CHINESE PROVERB

Powerful feelings help the writer to recall and record interesting material. You can experiment with strong, passionate single sentences by completing some sentences that are already started, such as these:

1. *I hate it when*
2. *I love it when*
3. *I don't think it's fair that*
4. *Why should I have to*
5. *It makes me laugh when*
6. *I cried when*
7. *Why do grown-ups always*
8. *My mother got mad when*

Finishing a sentence that was started by someone else is a good way to practice your writing. The beginning of the sentence gives you the push you need to get moving the way someone used to help you to swing when you were little. Once you got going, the momentum made it easier for you to keep moving. And as you got more practice, you didn't need someone to give you that first push. This is true with writing, too.

The second advantage of playing with these half-finished sentences is that their subject matter is pretty emotional, and most people find it easier to write about something that evokes powerful feelings. The strong beginnings usually make for even stronger endings, as in the following examples:

1. *I hate it when my sister's ice-cream cone lasts longer than mine.*
2. *I love it when my dog sneaks into bed with me.*
3. *I don't think it's fair that my parents can watch as much T.V. as they want to but I can't.*
4. *Why should I have to clean my room?*
5. *It makes me laugh when the teacher picks on someone else.*

6. *I cried when my friend's dog got her tongue caught in an old tuna-fish can.*
7. *Why do grown-ups always say, "Did you say hello to Mrs. So-and-So?"*
8. *My mother got mad when I pinched my sister.*

Now you try it. Go back to the started sentences, copy them onto a sheet of paper, and write an ending for each one.

Once you have written the endings, read over the sentences and choose the one you like best. Now find the biggest piece of blank paper you can, such as a page from an over-sized newsprint pad, get comfortable on the floor, and draw a picture to illustrate your favorite of the eight sentences. When the drawing is completed, write the sentence on the bottom of the page and sign your name.

Your single sentence is a powerful piece of communication by itself. Adding the drawing simply adds to its impact, making your message more important and complete. It will show you how much you can get across in one sentence. In fact, a single illustrated sentence can tell a little story. It might look like any of these:

I hate it when my sister's ice-cream cone lasts longer than mine.

Why should I have to eat hard-boiled eggs?

I love it when my dog sneaks into bed with me.

My mother got mad when I went out in the snow without my hat and boots.

Why do grown-ups always say, "Did you say hello to Mrs. So-and-So?"

You can create a mood and tell a story with a sentence. Starting small—by constructing interesting sentences and then illustrating them—you will soon be going on to bigger and better things, like writing books. The next chapter will show you how.

5

Creating Books

A book is like a garden carried in the pocket.

CHINESE PROVERB

If you have trouble coming up with good topics, intriguing opening sentences, interesting middles, or exciting conclusions, start small—write a small book.

First, construct the book from a sheet of unlined 8 1/2 x 11 paper. Fold your paper into sixteenths. You do this by folding it in half four times in a row. Now cut along the folds. This will give you sixteen pages that are each 2 3/4 x 2 1/8 inches. Staple your pieces along one side so that you have a little book that opens from the side or the bottom, depending on which way you want to hold it.

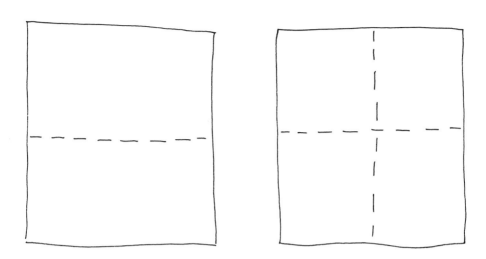

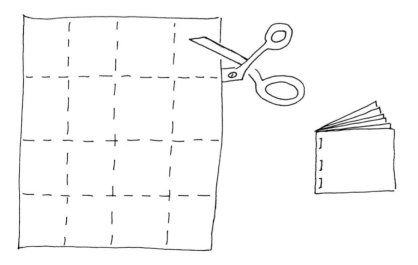

Now choose a theme. Having a theme will make it a snap to get ideas for your little book. Here are some examples:

1. *When I Grow Up*
2. *Happiness Is*
3. *It Makes Me Mad!*
4. *The Little Book of Dreams*
5. *The (Horse, Bicycle, Baseball, Dog, Stamp Collecting, Treasure Digging, Magic, Space) Book*

This time you will write several sentences (as many of them as you want), all of them on the same topic—the topic of your tiny book. After you write them and fix them up, copy them into your little book, one to a page, and illustrate each one with a tiny drawing. Think up a good title for your book—and put that on the cover with another tiny illustration. Your book might look like one of these:

Here are two pages from *The Little Book of Prehistoric Animals*:

Pterodactyls lived before there was T.V.

Stegosaurs were herbivorous.

Here are four pages from *Big Wishes in a Tiny Book*:

I wish I could visit the moon.

I wish I had a dog of my own.

I wish I could conduct an orchestra.

I wish I could sleep under the stars every night.

Instead of a tiny book, how would you like a H U G E one? You can make one out of pages from a large newsprint pad. Tear off six or eight or ten pages and staple them across the top to make your book. You can hold the book so that it opens from the bottom or the right.

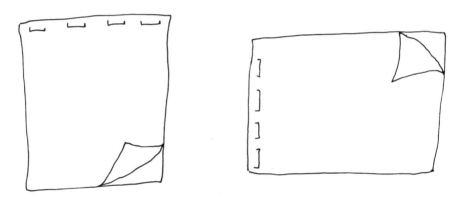

A theme will help you fill the book. Suppose your birthday is coming. You can write about all the presents you hope to get, or what life will be like now that you are one year older. You can tell the world about it in a gigantic book.

Write one sentence at the bottom of each page, and then do an enormous drawing in the rest of the space. Working large will make your work look very important—even if your subject is very, very small:

Here is a page from *Mice Are Nice*:

Some mice live in the city.

Think of a shape. Choose a theme. Write a book.

You can make books in any size or shape you like. You can make the world's skinniest book or the tallest one. You can write a fat book or a round one. Your book can be serious or silly, full of facts or full of fantasy. It can be designed to make people think or laugh or cry.

When you finish a small book and a huge book, there's another kind of book for you to make. The next chapter will tell you all about it.

A Writer's Notebook

I love being a writer. What I can't stand is the paperwork.

PETER DE VRIES

Your writing deserves to be kept together and saved. Begin a writer's notebook, in which you can store and preserve all your work. You can use a loose-leaf book filled with lined paper. Or you can make a book (like the ones you just made) by stapling together a pile of lined paper sandwiched in between two sheets of colored paper. Give your book a title. It can be something simple such as *My Writing* or any other title you like.

Now when you write, you can correct your work and then copy it over into your writer's notebook. (No writer gets it perfect the first time around.) Or you can write and edit right in your notebook, keeping a record of all the changes you make as you go along.

Make a safe place for your writing, too—part of a drawer, a spot on the bookshelf, a box near your bed—so that you always know where it is. Start saving your writing today. In just a few months, you'll be surprised to see how much you've written and how good your writing is.

Ah! Inspiration!

No army can withstand the strength of an idea whose time has come.

VICTOR HUGO

If writers wrote only when they were inspired, there would be hardly anything in the world to read. Instead of sitting around waiting for ideas to float in through the window, wouldn't it be grand if you could make inspiration happen whenever you wanted to write? Here's some good news: You can. And this chapter will show you how.

Suppose you had a list of topics to think about whenever you needed an idea for a story? These topics would serve as reminders, places to fish around in your memory whenever you were in need of inspiration. Such a list follows. Will each item work for *you*? Of course not. No matter. Some of them will work very well. Will each "story" you think of fit neatly into one of the topics the way a candy bar fits into your mouth? No—it won't. Some of the story ideas you get could fit into several of the topics. Therefore, you could use the hints under Reality, Reality (Doctored), Pets, Hobbies and Pastimes, or even Dreams to write about your dog, for example. That's good. It gives you lots of choices, lots of room to be yourself.

How can you use these topics? You can ask yourself some leading questions, such as:

Did I have any interesting dreams lately that might help me to write a good story?

Has anything happened to me lately that I could write about? Should I write about this event exactly as it occurred, or should I change the sequence, the characters, the outcome?

Would my pets or hobbies make a good story? Could I invent a good hobby or an unusual pet and write about it? Could I invent a whole world and write about it? (Why not!)

Did I have an absolutely weird or funny notion lately?

Is there some intriguing photograph I've seen that could help me write a story?

Could I write something, made-up or true-to-life, about a wild animal, a relative, a spaceman?

Now read on and see how you can make these topics work for you. You will also see how some other writers made them work for them.

Dreams

"Throw your dream into space like a kite, and you do not know what it will bring back..."

ANAÏS NIN

A dream can be an unusual and powerful inspiration for a story. If you don't usually remember your dreams, you can teach yourself to do so. Leave a pencil and paper near the bed. Then, before you fall asleep, remind yourself to recall your dreams. With practice, you will be able to remember the stories you "write" in your sleep and write them down as soon as you wake up.

When you write up your dream as a piece of fiction, you can change it. You can fill in the blank spots. You can write a new ending. You can add characters. And you do not have to write as if you are writing about a dream. The original dream is merely your inspiration, the thing that propels you into action. As you work with dreams, you'll find you are inventive and colorful in your sleep, just as you are when you are awake.

Here's how one bad dream became a good story:

The Devil

There was a hole in the floor. I was coming home from school when I fell in and there was a devil down there. The devil caught me. But he wasn't smart so when he went to sleep, I slipped through the bars and I found some cement. When I got out of the hole, I had an idea. I covered the hole with cement and my troubles were over with.

REBECCA LOBL (8)

Reality

Everything is funny as long as it is happening to somebody else.

WILL ROGERS

The best advice to any writer of any age is "Write about what you know." Using real life as the core of your story or poem will give you more information than you would ever need to use. Perhaps you've never been to Kansas or the moon or ridden on a subway in Brooklyn or sipped fine tea in the Casbah. But you have been in your house—and you know every corner of it, just as you know every bird and bush in your own neighborhood. You know the quirks and habits of your relatives and friends, don't you? More than that, you've had experience galore, some of which would make funny or sad or moving stories.

Any human can feel he's alone from time to time. Each of us, sometimes, feels he's the worst fool ever born, the only one in the history of the human race who doesn't know what every other human seems to know automatically. Writing the "truth" (even if it's not *exactly* as it happened) can make the reader feel he's not alone. Reading your story, he can feel he's not the only clod stumbling awkwardly through his life. That same story can help you to laugh at your troubles or enjoy your adventures all over again.

Here are some examples of writing inspired by reality:

Once when I was in the shower, I said, "I want milk! I want milk!!!" I said that about ten times. Then my mother brought me a glass of milk—in the shower, mind you—and I took one sip and said, "I don't want it anymore." Then my mother got so mad she spilled the whole thing on my head.

VICTORIA HALBOTH (10)

"Buddy," she said, "maybe you could be a writer."

I clasped the idea to my heart. I had never met a writer, had shown no previous urge to write, and hadn't a notion how to become a writer, but I loved stories and thought that making up stories must surely be almost as much fun as reading them. Best of all, though, and what really gladdened my heart, was the ease of the writer's life. Writers did not have to trudge through the town peddling from canvas bags, defending themselves against angry dogs, being rejected by surly strangers. Writers did not have to ring doorbells. So far as I could make out, what writers did couldn't even be classified as work.

RUSSELL BAKER, *Growing Up*

An Old Man Thinking About What He Hates

Hate is children who always get sick
With running noses that they pick
While they stuff their bellies
Perched by their tellies

And watch a stupid cartoon
From morning 'til noon.

Then Monday comes and they're off with their books
And pass my house with ugly eyes
I can't stand the little devils
They're like stinging flies.

LYNN OFFERMAN (11)

Reality (Doctored)

I am always at a loss to know how much to believe of my own stories.

WASHINGTON IRVING

Many writers tell stories that are loosely based on reality. However, once they begin to write, they deviate from the truth in order to make the story a product of their own imagination. Much of fiction is reality transformed to a greater or lesser degree. This allows writers to write about what they know and have experienced without losing their freedom to imagine, alter, add, and subtract. Doctoring reality gives you the best of both worlds—that which really occurred and that which you invent. Disguising the story also avoids embarrassing any of the people who were part of the real-life drama. In addition, by altering the "truth," a writer can make a story come out better than it did in reality.

So if your big brother always gets the best of you in real life, why should he be so privileged in your stories? If you have to go to bed early or your allowance is tiny, in your stories you can read until dawn and have your own checking account. *Your stories are yours.* As long as they *seem* real and possible, you can take them in any direction that pleases you. After all, telling the truth isn't the point—telling a good story is. How far from the facts you travel when writing fiction is entirely up to you.

Of course, if you are specifically asked to write truthfully about a subject, you should. But when the point is good writing, you can certainly be inventive. When in doubt, simply ask, "Does what I write have to be true?" You can even put the word "fiction" in parentheses under your title to make sure your reader understands what you are doing.

When a story is written well, it *sounds* real. How much of it may have actually happened, and to whom, is the author's business. No one else need ever know where the truth left off and make-believe began....

I'm just going to tell you the story the way it happened, and I'm afraid it's going to shock a few people. Most of what I'm going to confess has to do with when I was fifteen years old. But I'm sixteen now, so I'm not as demented as I was then.

PAUL ZINDEL, Confessions of a Teenage Baboon

One warm night in May, in the back of the hearse, while I was whispering, "I love you, I love you," into Lauralei Rabinowitz' soft, black hair, she said, "Stop right there, Wally! There are three reasons this can't go on any longer!"

"*Three* reasons?" I said.

"Three reasons," she said, sitting up, reaching into her blazer pocket for her comb. She combed her hair while she told me what they were.

"One," she said, "you're not Jewish."

"Two," she said, "you're shorter than I am."

"And three," she said, "you're going to be an undertaker."

M. E. KERR, I'll Love You When You're More Like Me

Once upon a time and a very good time it was there was a moocow coming down along the road and this moocow that was down along the road met a nicens little boy named baby tuckoo....

His father told him that story: his father looked at him through a glass: he had a hairy face.

JAMES JOYCE, A Portrait of the Artist As a Young Man

Sheer Fantasy

It was a bright cold day in April, and the clocks were striking thirteen.

GEORGE ORWELL, 1984

Everyone loves some kind of fantasy—fables; fairy tales; science fiction; action-packed, unrealistic adventures; talking animals; creatures from another galaxy; monsters; magic; or miracles.

If you write fantasy, you have to make it work. That is, within the context of the world you create, your characters and plot have to be believable. In a way, this makes good fantasy more difficult to write than good "reality." You not only have to make up a plot and characters, you have to make up all the ground rules, too.

If you like this genre, by all means take notes before you begin. In the world of your story, do animals talk? Is there gravity? What is the year—and why? Are we on earth? Who are the characters in the story, and what can and cannot they do? Has flight been invented? Do your characters need a plane or some other "gadget" in order to fly? Is there the automobile, the bathtub, Saran Wrap, the nectarine? If you decide ahead of time, you will be able to be consistent within your story. That will help to make your story good.

With good notes to refer to, you won't make Zook fly for the first time to get him out of a jam from which there is no escape *unless* you have clearly hinted to the reader that all *Nagucians* know how to fly. With proper planning, you won't paint yourself into the kind of corner that makes you end your story with, "And do you know what happened then? Guess." By making notes and being sure of what can and can't happen in your story (rabbits can talk but they can't fly, Marp can move objects simply by staring at them but he cannot read minds), you will be able to lay the groundwork for your plot and make all your startling surprises *seem* plausible. Here are some samples:

"And when you wake, everything you know of the

twentieth century will be gone from your mind. As you sleep, that entire body of knowledge will shrink in your mind; it will dwindle to a motionless pinpoint deep in your brain, and lost to you.

"It's beginning to happen now. There are no such things as automobiles, Si; there are no planes, computers, television, no world in which they are possible. 'Nuclear' and 'electronics' appear in no dictionary anywhere on the face of the earth."

JACK FINNEY, Time and Again

…he moved impulsively forward, and holding out his hand grasped mine with a strength which made me wince, an effect which was not lessened by the fact that it seemed as cold as ice—more like the hand of a dead than a living man.

BRAM STOKER, Dracula

There was a count. He was hanging around Newark, New Jersey. He got out of his coffin and flew to someone's window. He bit an old lady in the neck. Then he flew to an old graveyard and he dug up Boris. He dug up Frankenstein. He dug up Babe Ruth by mistake. They

had a Bloody Mary and Bat's Milk to celebrate Hallo-
ween. The count, Frankenstein, and Boris said, "Pray for
the dead and the dead will pray for you."

MICHAEL KRIEG (8)

Pets

Writing is a dog's life, but the only life worth living.

GUSTAVE FLAUBERT

The combination of knowledge plus affection makes
writing about pets both powerful and touching. When you do
a piece of prose or poetry about your pet, it is best if you can
observe the pet while you are writing. Noting the tiniest details
of appearance and behavior will give your work verisimilitude
(the appearance of truth) and enable your readers to see the
animal as if they were right there with you.

Once you have the appearance and behavior of your pet
down pat, you can choose whether you want to write a story
about the animal in which you make up the events, or if your
piece will be nonfiction, an essay describing behavior or true
events. In either case, here are some useful tips for writing
about pets:

1. Write as a natural scientist, using careful, patient observation of appearance and behavior:

The Gerbils

Every time I walk into my room, the five gerbils in the big cage put their big ears up. Then some of them get on top of their wheel and stand on their hind legs. The other ones just stand on their hind legs to see who is there.

In another cage is Sally. Sally likes to chew up everything. She chewed up my shirts. She chewed up my wash cloth. She chewed up my shower curtain and my floor mat.

Martin is a fat gerbil. Martin likes to stand on top of his wheel and wait for me to come into the room.

Horace is a little gerbil. He likes to run on the floor and run in his wheel. He is always running around. Whenever I put Horace on the floor, he runs around. He would only stop for one sunflower seed.

The two fat hamsters are always sleeping. They are only making noise in the night. They always want to be fed. They both have big ears, long whiskers and a little bit of red hair.

ANDY WEISS (10)

2. *Display your affection without sentimentality:*

My hamster, how I love her
I'm always thinking of her
Everybody thinks she's cute
Nice and small and sweet to boot
Never has she made me sad
Every day she makes me glad
Mienne's not a mouse or a rat
You should never call her that
Hamster, hamster, that she is
And her tail is hers, not his
My mom still can't get that straight
Still she says that "he" is great
Tender love she gives for free, 'n'
Everything I love she's bein'
Really love my little Mienne.

JENNIFER LENNARD (15)

NOTE: READ THIS POEM ACROSTICALLY (THE FIRST LETTER OF EACH LINE GOING DOWN)
IN ORDER TO FIND THE HIDDEN TITLE.

3. Be specific. Small details are your strongest assets:

Bosco

He smells with his nose.
And he makes a tic-tic sound with his toes.
When he's comfortable he sits,
After he's had a convincing sniff.

KATHY WEINERT (11)

4. When writing fiction or fantasy about a pet, think about the writing tips in "Sheer Fantasy" as well as those in this section.

"Fiver?" said the other rabbit. "Why's he called that?"

"Five in the litter, you know: he was the last—and the smallest. You'd wonder nothing had got him by now. I always say a man couldn't see him and a fox wouldn't want him. Still, I admit he seems to be able to keep out of harm's way."

The small rabbit came closer to his companion, lolloping on long hind legs.

"Let's go a bit further, Hazel," he said. "You know,

there's something queer about the warren this evening, although I can't tell exactly what it is. Shall we go down to the brook?"

"All right," answered Hazel, "and you can find me a cowslip. If you can't find one, no one can."

RICHARD ADAMS, Watership Down

A Weird Notion

I'm not afraid to die. I just don't want to be there when it happens.

WOODY ALLEN

Sometimes you'll get a funny idea—a notion that might someday make the heart of a good story. Jot it down. Start a file of weird notions.

Perhaps you have wondered how something ordinary first began—how salad was invented, who caught the first fish, or how singing started. Maybe you'd like to know where squirrels sleep—and in what positions—or how the boxer dog got its pushed-in nose, or what man's greatest invention was. Great. Maybe your answer would make a funny story.

What if your weird notion is just a sentence that gets stuck

51

in your head like a tune? This happens to writers all the time. They have characters searching for stories, titles looking for plots, middles that need beginnings and ends. Keep the weird notion in your weird notion file. One day it may bloom into a complete and amusing story.

Your file might include notes like these:

Talking vegetables—what would they talk about?
How did someone get the idea for television??
An advice column: on what? written by whom?

Your weird notion might develop into a story.

A Good Idea

There was a caveman and he wanted to cross a river because his friend was on the other side. So he dug out a log and paddled across. When he got there he could not find his friend. He looked high and low and then he found his friend. Then he ate fish with his friend. And his friend asked him how he got across the river. He said, "I dug out a log and paddled across." His friend said, "I think you have discovered the boat."

ROBBIE DEWEY (10)

Ralph

Ralph was a purebred Scandinavian alligator, one of the rarest kind of reptiles. He won every alligator show he was in. He also won every reptile show he was in, until a big, mean, old witch put a spell on Ralph and turned him into an itty-bitty Welsh pony. Poor Ralph! No more alligator shows. He was depressed. So he bucked everybody who mounted him. And his owners put him in the pasture where there was an apple tree to kick and get out his anger. But he jumped the fence because the apple tree looked like the old witch. It had a squirrel hole that looked like her mouth and twisted, curvy limbs like her hair. But mostly what scared him were the stumps where two huge branches had been cut off. And all together it had more than a slight resemblance to the witch.

The groom caught him and yelled, "Dumb horse. You're like an alligator," and as fast as you can say, "One, two, three," Ralph was an alligator again, a prize-winning, purebred, Scandinavian alligator. And he hurried home so as not to miss dinner.

BETSY EHRENFELD (12)

53

When Mrs. Frederick C. Little's second son was born, everyone noticed that he was not much bigger than a mouse. The truth of the matter was, the baby looked very much like a mouse in every way. He was only about two inches high; and he had a mouse's sharp nose, a mouse's tail, a mouse's whiskers, and the pleasant, shy manner of a mouse. Before he was many days old he was not only looking like a mouse but acting like one, too—wearing a gray hat and carrying a small cane.

E. B. WHITE, Stuart Little

Hobbies and Pastimes

A man is only as good as what he loves.

SAUL BELLOW

Are you the world's leading authority on anything? Do you have a hobby, a passion, a pastime? Are you simply *nuts* about baseball, old movies, the solar system, dinosaurs, magic tricks, jogging, hairy dogs, military costumes? Is it horses, horses, horses, all day long? Do you collect things— maps, things from the sea, old coins? Kid, have I got news for you! Write about what you know.

An Appaloosa

An Appaloosa has a spotted rump
With ears that tell him to jump.
He touches things with his nose
And likes to be squirted with a hose.

He can walk, trot and canter
In a very smooth manner.
He eats grass, hay and oats
To help grow his winter coats.

BETSY EHRENFELD (11)

Write with detail. Write with clarity. Write with affection.

In truth, Ernie does bark, but it is never grating, is almost always done outdoors, and will change depending on whether he is working or playing. His bark is most often used as a friendly greeting to children, dogs and cats to come play with him. His bark sets off the wagging tail quite nicely.

BRUCE HAROLD WOLK, "Tracking Down a Rare Breed"

And if you are teaching others how to do the thing you do (write music, keep fish, build model cars, knit), make sure that your directions and instructions are full and informative and easy to follow.

Swiss Chocolate Cookies

$2/3$ cup butter ($1\frac{1}{3}$ sticks)

1 cup sugar

1 egg

2 1-ounce squares
 unsweetened
 chocolate, melted

$2\frac{1}{2}$ cups all-purpose flour

1 teaspoon baking powder

$\frac{1}{2}$ teaspoon salt

$\frac{1}{4}$ teaspoon cinnamon

$1/3$ cup milk

1 teaspoon vanilla

Soften butter and beat in sugar, egg, and chocolate. Combine dry ingredients and add alternately with milk and vanilla, mixing well after each addition.

Roll out $\frac{1}{8}$ inch thick on lightly floured surface and cut into desired shapes. Place on oiled baking sheets and bake at 400° for 5–7 minutes.

Makes about 5 dozen cut-outs.

ANNE SERANNE, *The Joy of Giving Homemade Food*

Wild Animals and Nature

You can observe a lot just by watching.

YOGI BERRA

Do you have a favorite animal at the zoo? Could you spend hours watching the elephants munch hay, the bears cavort in their pond, the monkeys playing just like kids? Do you love trees, fields of corn, waterfalls?

Nature and her creatures move many a writer to grab a pen and pad and let the words come pouring out. When this happens to you, here are some steps to take before you write:

1. Research: Get the facts and slip them into your narrative to make your story seem real. How does your animal capture its dinner? Does it mate for life? Do its colors change with the seasons? What is its natural habitat? Now you can place the animal where it belongs and have it behave as a real member of its species would. Now you have the choice. You can write fiction about animals, making up a story in which the animals behave as real animals would. You can write nonfiction, recording a true incident in which an animal plays an important role, or in which you describe some animal's behavior, habits, etc. Or you can write fantasy (see that section) by changing one or two or three things about the behavior of the animal in order to make the story conform to what you have in mind.

2. *Observe: You can watch wild animals at the zoo. You can observe nature all around you,* in the plant that grows on your windowsill, in the tree that grows up between the cracks in a city sidewalk, in the rolling meadow alive with wild flowers, birds, beasts, and insects, in the stream that runs by your house. Expand your research with your eyes, seeing things better than you did before you became a writer. Writing, like carrots, is good for the vision.

3. *Record: Write down things you want to savor and save for a story.* Sometimes a word or phrase will remind you of how something looked or smelled or felt. These specifics will make what you are describing seem to come to life for your reader.

4. *Imagine: Even though you will want to describe wild animals and nature with a hawk-eyed accuracy and a richness of detail, you need not leave your imagination behind.* Once nature is behaving in the way she must, you can make up events and adventures that will make your story a page turner.

Sometimes you can offer your reader clarity and understanding by comparing the thing you are writing about to something else, something perhaps more familiar to your reader. Saying one thing is like another adds a new dimension to your description. It offers the reader, in a way, a new way to see:

> A brook is an unharnessed thing
> It seems to be able to take wing.
>
> BETSY EHRENFELD (11)

An Elephant

Your nose we call a trunk.
You're just a large gray hunk.
Your legs are stiff gray trees.
The knotholes are your wrinkled knees.
Your ears, as we can see,
Are the leaves of this great tree.
Your tusks are two white boughs.
You're all like trees—bulls and cows.

CELIA CONVERSE (10)

On the other hand, you can also paint an excellent portrait by contrasting two things, by illuminating their opposite qualities:

City and Country

Streams, brooks and rivers run smoothly.
Trees, bushes and weeds wave roundly.
Trucks, cars and buses run roughly.
Curtains, flags and papers wave loudly.

SARAH THOMAS (11)

Whatever way you choose to write about nature, don't forget to put your heart into what you write:

The handler opened the lid and there, lying on a blanket of shredded newspapers, was an adorable and frightened baby chimpanzee. Dark chocolate eyes were set in a light mocha face that was as soft as doeskin, and on his chin was a powder-white fuzz of a beard. His hair was silky and black and parted in the center of his head, bristling out at the sides around two outrageously comic big ears. Something this cute could not be real. It was undoubtedly a very ingenious battery-operated toy. Somewhere on his underside there had to be a tag that said "Made in Japan." But suddenly I was holding him and there was no tag in sight. In one magic moment he threw his arms around my neck, thoroughly wet my coat, and, though I did not know it then, totally annihilated a lifetime of rationality and logic.

HESTER MUNDIS, *No He's Not a Monkey, He's an Ape and He's My Son*

Photographs

A photograph is a secret about a secret....

DIANE ARBUS

A photograph can be an insurance policy against going blank when you try to write. Remember the proverb "One picture is worth more than ten thousand words"? Studying a picture can help you find some of those thousands of words for your story.

Hold a photograph in your hands. Become acquainted. Note the setting, perhaps the time of day. What is in the background? Is there a person, an animal in the photograph? How does he look—thoughtful, happy, frightened, tired, secretive, sly, mean, sad, sweet? Why might he look that way? Now you're collecting the meat and potatoes for a

Photo: Carol Lea Benjamin

62

story. What may have happened before the photo was taken? What might be about to occur? Remember, the picture is only inspiration. The story is yours to imagine and invent.

Making up a story inspired by a photograph is fascinating to do, because it gets you to look at, and then beyond, the surface. As your eye and then your mind examines the photo, as you learn to see *in*, you are teaching yourself to see more, something *every* writer needs to do. A writer cannot stop at just the surface. He must learn to dip beneath, to ask himself *why* and to come up with plausible answers.

Refugee of the Rain

He was born in a box in the rain,
A little ways off the sandy lane,
Wanted by none was this ball of fur,
To others he was a filthy cur.
But not to me, a boy in the rain,
Walking upon this sandy, wet lane.
I came across Steve, as I called him;
To take him home was my greatest whim.
But I left Steve there, 'cause mother hates dogs,
And I walked alone through the dark, gray fogs.

I shall always remember that day,
For at a dog show in the month of May,
A champion won the blue ribbon;
Believe me, I'm not kiddin',
I recognized this ball of brown fluff,
Now full-grown, and called "Champion Ruff."
Yes it was Steve, others' pet peeve,
The refugee of the rain.

CAROL KAHN (10)

What might you write after studying this photograph?

Photo: Carol Lea Benjamin

Or this one?

Photo: Noah A. Kahn

Or this one?

Photo: Stephen Lennard

Practice making up stories from photographs whenever you get the chance. You might find an interesting one in an ad on the bus, while waiting to eat in a restaurant, or on a poster you pass in the street. There are photographs everywhere—and the clever writer can make use of them.

Someday you might get stuck in school when you are supposed to write a composition. Look around the room. Find a photograph that will help you get started. Or even close your eyes and imagine your favorite picture—your grandparents together and smiling, your dog retrieving a stick, some cows in a pasture, a daredevil pilot. Now you will be able to weave a story around that image.

More Things to Do:

1. *In your writer's notebook, begin to keep a list of dreams you can remember.* Some of them may be nightmares! Fine. You can make a great horror story out of a bad dream—or you can rewrite the ending and make a bad start finish well. Try to turn one of your dreams into a story.

2. *Take your notebook out for a walk.* Find an animal to observe and describe. (You don't have to live on a farm to do this. Nature is everywhere.)

Pigeon

When a pigeon moves around
He bobs his head up and down.
He likes bread crumbs especially
He'll beg for them for you and me.
A pigeon's beak is also his nose
And on each foot he has three toes.

CELIA CONVERSE (10)

3. *Try to think of something that was absolutely awful when it happened to you but that, looking back, would make a funny story.* Now write that story in your writer's notebook.

4. *Go through your family album and look at the pictures in a new way.* Think about the secrets hidden in each one, secrets you could "uncover" in your stories. Ask if you can have one of the photos for your writer's notebook, and try to write a story about what you see in the picture. Then keep the photo in your notebook with your story.

What I Did on My Summer Vacation

What's in a name? That which we call a rose
By any other name would smell as sweet.

WILLIAM SHAKESPEARE, *Romeo and Juliet*

What student breathes who has never been asked to write a composition entitled "What I Did on My Summer Vacation," "A Day I'll Never Forget," or "My Hobby"? Pretitled school assignments can be tough on any writer. But learning how to make any notion that interests you, or any form of inspiration, fit the title you are given can result in a terrific story that is fun to write instead of giving you a terrible case of writer's block.

A long time ago, I was asked to write a composition entitled "My Hobby." I really wanted to do well. Unfortunately, I didn't *have* a hobby. Therefore, on first glance, I decided the topic was stupid and boring. But then I got an idea. I made up a hobby—a good one—and wrote about it realistically, as if I were writing the absolute truth. I wrote that my hobby was making robots—and I told all about how I made them in the basement of my house. I filled the composition with believable details about how and when I worked at constructing my robots out of saved and flattened tin cans. I even listed, most carefully, what the robots could and couldn't do. The ploy worked and I received a good grade.

What should *you* do when you have to satisfy a pretitled assignment in school:

You can write about something real and stick pretty much to the truth.

You can alter the truth, fictionalizing a real event. In this case, change the names of the people and write "fiction" on your story to avoid confusion.

You can make fantasy sound realistic, writing about something made up as if it were the bald truth. If you think you'll confuse your teacher, you can mark it "fiction."

Something that interests you, that entertains you, would make good material for a composition. Almost anything, with a little thinking, can be made to fit the title on the blackboard.

Suppose *you* have a hobby. But the topic you are given is "A Day I'll Never Forget." Great. Write about your first stamp show or the day your first model plane flew or the day you found your first Indian-head nickel. Suppose, like me, you don't have a hobby and the title is "My Hobby." Do you know enough about some hobby to write about it as if it were yours? Can you make up a wild and fascinating hobby and write about it in an entertaining way—raising and breeding hamsters, teaching mynah birds to talk, charting the constellations, nature photography?

Here are some more examples of how a little imagination can give flexibility to a pretitled assignment:

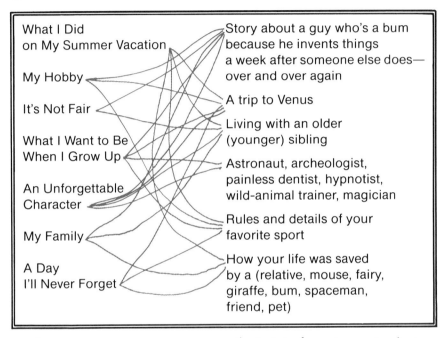

What I Did on My Summer Vacation

My Hobby

It's Not Fair

What I Want to Be When I Grow Up

An Unforgettable Character

My Family

A Day I'll Never Forget

Story about a guy who's a bum because he invents things a week after someone else does— over and over again

A trip to Venus

Living with an older (younger) sibling

Astronaut, archeologist, painless dentist, hypnotist, wild-animal trainer, magician

Rules and details of your favorite sport

How your life was saved by a (relative, mouse, fairy, giraffe, bum, spaceman, friend, pet)

As you can see, you can neatly twist almost any topic to fit the title on the blackboard. After all, telling the truth is not the issue—telling a good story is. And finding an exciting topic to fit the bill will help you to write a good story.

The message is this: Even when someone else writes the title, you still have choices, you still have room in which to be imaginative, you can still enjoy the act of writing.

Wonderful Words

"When I use a word," Humpty Dumpty said in rather a scornful tone, 'it means just what I choose it to mean—neither more nor less."

"The question is," said Alice, "whether you *can* make words mean so many different things."

"The question is," said Humpty Dumpty, "which is to be master—that's all."

LEWIS CARROLL, *Through the Looking Glass*

When you were just learning to talk, you loved each new word you mastered. You understood and appreciated the power of words, being aware, after a brief practice period, that "more" got you a second helping and that "up" got you carried aloft. You knew that "no" was sturdy and serviceable, that "yes" often made people smile. The results you got had to do with the specific message each word conveyed, the command it issued, the affirmation or denial it offered, the image it evoked. It had to do with definition.

As a writer, you will once again pay careful attention to the meanings of the words you choose to use. By doing so, you will be able to add clarity, vigor, color, and humor to your writing. Of course, when your writing is flowing well, you will just want to keep it moving. But afterwards you can begin to think about the important words; you can then check out their exact meanings in your dictionary. In this way, you will make your writing much more varied and interesting—and you will increase the number of words of which you are the master.

Finding just the right word for the job is part of the fun of writing. Doing this will also help your readers know exactly what you are trying to say. In order to do this, you must make friends with your dictionary.

A dictionary is a writer's best tool. It contains all the words you can imagine—and many you can't—each properly spelled and clearly defined. You can take an ordinary story and make it soar by replacing the shopworn words with fresh ones.

The difference between the right word and the almost right word is the difference between lightning and the lightning bug.

MARK TWAIN

When you look up a word, never rush. Let your eyes wander on the page. In that way, for the same trouble, you may learn two or even three new words, words that will make your writing stronger, richer, more persuasive, funnier. Most important, you will be gathering the information that will help you to communicate, not to confuse.

Once you establish the habit of looking for the most accurate word in order to make your point or paint your word picture, you will also discover (or rediscover, since surely this is something, too, that every baby knows) that words can be wonderful for reasons other than definitions—because, for instance, of the way they *sound.*

Buzz, boom, and *cuckoo* sound like what they mean. This phenomenon is called onomatopoeia, a pretty fantastic-sounding word itself: ahn-uh-mah-tuh-*pee*-yuh.

I also like to use words that are just plain fun to say—*drizzle, roseola, sauerbraten, lollypop.*

Some words have great looks. When I can, I like to slip some terrific-looking words into my narrative, words like *ooze*, *oops*, and *pterodactyl*.

Practice, Practice

The more you learn about words, the more you'll love them. So practice, practice:

1. *Add two new lovable words a week to your writer's notebook. You may have to read twenty to find the right two. Then spell them correctly and write their meanings next to them. By the time you use them three times, they'll be yours forever.*
2. *Using your dictionary, find a word that looks funny. Find a word that sounds terrific.*
3. *Words like* swivel, pseudonym, metamorphosis, *and* replica *have such specific meanings that they add clarity to your writing whenever you use them. Can you find two more words with narrow meanings in your dictionary?*
4. *Be a dictionary detective. Look in as many different*

dictionaries as you can find—at home, in the library, in the bookstore. What's in the front, before the definitions start? What's in the back, after the z words? A dictionary is a fine place for a treasure hunt.

5. Consulting your dictionary, replace each of the underlined words in the following paragraph with a more wonderful one (note: some of the new words may be bigger; others may be smaller):

Scarlet is truly a <u>nice</u> dog. She can be <u>aloof</u> with strangers. But once she gets to know someone, she is very <u>affectionate.</u> In fact, she can deliver so much <u>mindfulness</u> that you may find yourself wishing she'd get <u>tired</u> and <u>surrender.</u>

Sentence to Paragraph to Finished Piece

Architecture should be dedicated to keeping the outside out and the inside in.

LEONARD BASKIN

At this point, you might be wondering just exactly how to go about constructing a sound story. There are as many different ways to do this as there are writers. You might want to begin at the beginning. (Not all writers do. But more about that later.) Here are three possible things you can accomplish with your opening sentence:

1. *You can set the stage.*

All nights should be so dark, all winters so warm, all headlights so dazzling.

MARTIN CRUZ SMITH, Gorky Park

I had a farm in Africa, at the foot of the Ngong Hills.

ISAK DINESEN, *Out of Africa*

There was once a very unbeautiful, very rocky, rotten island.

WILLIAM STEIG, *The Bad Island*

2. *You can introduce a character.*

Emma Inch looked no different from any other middle-aged, thin woman you might glance at in the subway or deal with across the counter of some small store in a country town, and then forget forever.

JAMES THURBER, *"The Departure of Emma Inch"*

You can make computers that are almost human.

LEWIS THOMAS, *The Lives of a Cell*

3. *You can state a conflict that will be dealt with in your story.*

My father stopped living with us when I was three or four.

FRANK CONROY, *Stop-Time*

Happy families are all alike; every unhappy family is unhappy in its own way.

LEO TOLSTOY, *Anna Karenina*

Standing before the kitchen sink and regarding the bright brass faucets that gleamed so far away, each with a bead of water at its nose, slowly swelling, falling, David again became aware that this world had been created without thought of him.

HENRY ROTH, *Call It Sleep*

Now you may ask, Should the first sentence of my story be long—

If you really want to hear about it, the first thing you'll probably want to know is where I was born, and what my lousy childhood was like, and how my parents were occupied and all before they had me, and all that David Copperfield kind of crap, but I don't feel like going into it, if you want to know the truth.

J. D. SALINGER, *The Catcher in the Rye*

short—

Nobody could sleep.

NORMAN MAILER, *The Naked and the Dead*

serious—

It was dark at six and the wind was blowing hard down East Broadway, where Marcus Rosenbloom stood near the bus stop waiting for his mother to come home from work.

HARRY MAZER, *The Dollar Man*

detailed—

My lifelong involvement with Mrs Dempster began at 5.58 o'clock p.m. on 27 December 1908, at which time I was ten years and seven months old.

ROBERTSON DAVIES, *Fifth Business*

depressing—

At the onset of the 1930s, my disillusionment with myself reached a stage in which I had lost all hope.

ISAAC BASHEVIS SINGER, *Lost in America*

informative—

Babar, the young King of the elephants, and his wife, Queen Celeste, have just left for their wedding trip in a balloon.

JEAN DE BRUNHOFF, *The Travels of Babar*

or fantastic—

In a hole in the ground there lived a hobbit.

J.R.R. TOLKIEN, *The Hobbit*

These points are all a matter of individual style. In fact, you may well begin one story with a long sentence that sets both mood and stage for what's to follow, and then begin your next story with a short sentence that introduces a character—and so on. There is no one best way. What is important is that whichever way you decide to begin, your first sentence compels the reader to continue reading. It sharpens interest about what is yet to come.

But what *is* to come? How will you, the writer, know where to go with your story once you have written the great American lead sentence?

By asking and answering some of the following questions, you will be able to flesh out your good lead into a strong, informative middle and eventually wind up with a moving, satisfying ending.

1. *Why is this (the statement in your first sentence) so and how does it reveal itself to the reader?*
2. *What will the character do to solve this problem?*
3. *Will he be successful? Will he have help—and if so, from whom—or will he be on his own?*
4. *Does the character learn anything during the course of the story? Does she change or grow up in any way? Will*

she gain revenge? Will she pay for her actions? Will she fail because of her own greed or pettiness? Will she succeed because she is independent, clever, energetic, lucky or resourceful?

5. What is the best way for this story to end? What ending is most in keeping with reality, with the character's personality, with the character's abilities and limitations, with the message (if there is one) of the story?

Constructing an interesting lead sentence and then asking questions is one way to get started and keep going. Not every writer works this way. Some writers write their first sentence *last*, polishing it and rewriting it, perfecting it, after all else is done. Still others think up a whole plot before putting one word on paper. You might work like this, too. If you do, brainstorming about your story can still be of help. It can help you to make sure you have answered all the important questions your reader will be asking as he or she reads. It can help you flesh out the plot and add essential details. It can even help you to come up with a good, solid ending.

What if one day you come up with a great ending for a story but no beginning or middle? Ask yourself some leading questions. You may be able to lead yourself backward all the way to the beginning.

1. *How did we get here?*
2. *Did the hero manage this all alone—or was help available?*
3. *When and where did the events begin that culminated in this exciting conclusion?*
4. *What kind of a character would it take to wind up in the situation that exists at the end of this story?*

What if you want to write a factual essay instead of a story? In this event, before you brainstorm about the details of your piece, get the facts. Once you have completed your research, then make sure you assemble the information in a logical fashion. Loaded down with the information you need about your particular subject, you will be able to explain, persuade, teach, incite. Now as you write, you can question yourself. Am I presenting the facts in the right order for this piece? Am I careful about showing both sides of an issue? Am I sticking to one point in each paragraph and not jumping around from fact to fact? Am I adding enough details and description for my reader to see things as I do? Brainstorming can help you write both fiction and nonfiction.

Here are some additional points to keep in mind as you build your story or essay:

1. *Keep it moving.*
2. *Make it sound true, even if it is.* Sometimes it is more difficult to make a true story sound real because things are so familiar to you that you forget to get them out of your head and onto the paper. When writing about people and events that are real, be extra careful to take the time to describe characters and events thoroughly.
3. *Don't add more characters—or issues—than you can handle.* Each character should be a recognizable individual with his or her own clear voice and an important role. Each issue you explore in an essay should be fully explained and backed up by facts.
4. *Don't show off.* Facts can help your story seem real. But make sure when you inject information into a story that it is there to make the story better and not merely to show the world how much you know. When you do research for either fiction or nonfiction, you will almost always accumulate more facts than you will need for your piece. When deciding how much information to include in story, essay, or poem, what's right for the

piece is what really counts.

5. *Sometime before your final draft, check the spellings and definitions of any words of which you are unsure. Correct your grammar, too.* Poor use of the language will weaken any piece of writing.

6. *Stick to what you know—or do a little research.* Inaccuracies break the mood of a story. It's easy enough to find out if horses eat hamburgers, if it snows in Georgia or how long it takes to get to the moon. Finding out is part of the fun of being a writer. And remember, research does not only mean looking in books. Research is looking and doing and asking questions and smelling and touching and tasting.

Private Writing: Keeping a Journal

How can I know what I think till I see what I say?

E. M. FORSTER

I often quote myself. It adds spice to my conversation.

GEORGE BERNARD SHAW

A journal or a diary is made up of private, daily writing. Of course, you may decide to show your journal to someone else from time to time. And you may not write absolutely every day. But the intent and the feel of the journal depend upon the fact that it is written regularly and not meant for anyone but you.

Why would you want to keep a journal? Why, indeed, would you want to write things that you didn't intend to share with anyone else? For all those good reasons named and illustrated in chapter two: to help remember important things, to clarify thoughts and sort out feelings, to express emotions in a safe way and then feel better for having done so, to outline plans or ideas, to hang on to impressions that would otherwise fade, to play with words, for fun, to gain satisfaction from self-expression, and just to see what happens as a piece of writing proceeds.

Some of what you can learn from keeping a journal is rather mysterious. You won't know what it is until you do it. That is, you know things—about yourself, about other people, about the world—that you do not realize you know. When you write, things come to light that, for some reason, do not do so when you talk or think or daydream. The act of writing brings them out. When you read your journal back to yourself, you will be suprised at how smart, thoughtful, and insightful you are.

Why write daily? Writing in a journal or diary every day helps take the pain out of writing. It becomes part of the ritual of your day to write in your journal. It's not a big deal, the way an important composition in school might seem. Therefore, writing becomes easier. Your writing will flow. This will help you anytime you have to write for any other reason. It also feels good to write every day, once you get started.

Why private writing? When you write for your eyes only,

you will be free to say precisely what you think and feel, as you can be in no other circumstances. You will not be limited or hampered or impeded by the thought that anyone else will read and judge your writing, thinking you mean or stupid or petty or false or less than clever or weird. In fact, when all is down on paper, you may even judge yourself less harshly. You get angry or confused. You make mistakes—even when you see them coming. You are sometimes petty and selfish and mean and grouchy. Yet you are also sweet and honest and you care about others. Sometimes you are afraid. Who isn't? Sometimes you are insightful, brave, and funny. In short, you are human— and the specific way in which you are will come out in your journal, making the keeping of a journal a very special experience.

It is handy, orderly, and private to keep your journal in a book. I use a loose-leaf notebook because I type my journal, then punch three holes in each page and insert it in the notebook. I make it a habit not to read what I have written for at least a week, sometimes two. Then, when my writing has "cooled off," I am able to learn from it, and I enjoy reading it back.

My habit is to write for five or ten minutes before going to sleep. In that way, if something is troubling me, I empty my troubles onto the page and sleep more peacefully. But of course you may write wherever, whenever, and in whatever pleases you.

A book of any sort is great because it is portable. You may like to write in bed or carry your book outside and sit under a tree, all alone, to work on your journal.

What topics should your journal contain? What style should you adopt? May you write about events one day and feelings the next? May you draw pictures to go along with the text or paste things into your journal—menus, report cards, letters, leaves, and petals, your puppy's baby teeth, movie ticket stubs? Do exactly and only as *you* wish. Your journal is yours. It is meant to please only you. Let it do so.

Here are some sample journals, illustrating the tremendous variety in how they can be done. The first was written about an experience in day camp:

I Really Did It

Dear Diary: Day One

I was afraid to even go in the pool. I haven't been in the water up to my head for who knows how long. My counselor said he would help me in the small pool but I was still scared.

Dear Diary: Day Two

I'm learning to swim, really, and fast too. Today I learned to kick, dunk and bob. I know I am doing good but I am still a little nervous.

Dear Diary: Day Three

Swimming is becoming more fun. Today I learned the Dead Man's Float. It was very scary. I had to keep my face in the water for 10 seconds and keep kind of stiff.

Dear Diary: Day Four

I *jumped* in the water. I REALLY DID IT! At first it seemed like such a hard thing to do, it took a lot of courage to try. My counselor said I am doing great.

Dear Diary: Day Five

I was Dead Man's Floating when I said to myself if I kicked and moved my arms I'll be swimming. I tried it and it worked. I was so happy. I finally learned to swim. I could even doggie paddle. Swimming is FUN!

Now I can get places in the water. I got my flying fish card at flagpole, and I was so glad.

On the bus ride home, I thought about the week and how great it was to learn to swim at Ramapo.

T.J. SIEGAL *(8)*

This next journal was done at a sleep-away camp:

> I wish that I was home
> I wish that I was magic.
> I wish that I had a thousand true friends.
> I wish that I knew everything.
> I wish that I was the most beautiful girl in the world.
> I wish that I had my mother right here.
> I wish that I was in school.
> I wish that it was Spring.
> I wish that I was grown-up.
> I wish that I had friends that were on T.V. shows.
> I wish there was children's liberation.
> I wish that I had all the candy in the world.
> I wish that I had a million comic books.
> I wish this page would come to an end.
> I wish my Grandfather was alive.
>
> JENNIFER LENNARD *(8)*

And last, this most famous diary written by a young Jewish girl in hiding from the Nazis during World War II:

> Into hiding—where would we go, in a town or the country, in a house or a cottage, when, how, where…?

These were the questions I was not allowed to ask, but I couldn't get them out of my mind. Margot and I began to pack some of our most vital belongings into a school satchel. The first thing I put in was this diary, then hair curlers, handkerchiefs, schoolbooks, a comb, old letters; I put in the craziest things with the idea that we were going into hiding. But I'm not sorry, memories mean more to me than dresses.

ANNE FRANK, *The Diary of a Young Girl*

Professional Secrets
You Can Use

Less is more.

ROBERT BROWNING

No writer gets it perfect the first time around.

Many professional writers write and then put their work away to cool before they try to improve it by editing. Being objective about your own work takes time—that is, there has to be some time between the writing and the fixing up.

Here are some of the tricks professional writers use to improve their own writing. You can use them too.

    1. *Let it cool.* When the emotions and the words are flowing, stick with that flow. After your story is finished, don't read it back for an hour, a day, or a week, depending upon how much time you can afford to wait. When your story is fresh, everything in it will look

wonderful. After some time, you will be able to see what is really good and what isn't.

2. *Look it over.* Now read your story over and see what's wrong with it. Are there mistakes? Can you add anything? Are some parts slow, dull, boring? Can you make them quick and funny? This is the time to rewrite, polish and edit. This is the time to make the bad good.

3. *Listen to the sound of it.* Read your story out loud. Mistakes you didn't see you may hear. The ear is a wonderful editor, helping you to weed out awkward sentences, long, dull passages, clumsy wording. Always take the time to edit by ear.

4. *Visualize it.* After the three initial editing stages—wait, read, and listen—read the story again, this time trying to *see* exactly what the story describes. (Be careful not to let yourself fill in the blanks.) Now you will discover which details are in your mind but not yet on paper. If you were thinking about your old black Cocker Spaniel, Fish, the comical fellow with the funny walk and the uneven ears, but you wrote only "dog," your reader can picture only *dog*. Did you want a generic animal in your story? Certainly not. If you rewrite your no-frills descriptions, your readers will *see* Fish—or

anything else—almost as well as you can.

By visualizing, you may also find people driving away without getting into the car, or walking through walls. I once discovered that I had someone holding a Twinkie and then covering her face with her hands without putting it down! Until I tried to see exactly what I had written, the poor character was smashing a Twinkie into her face right in the school cafeteria. Visualizing can help you to be clear, correct, and specific.

5. *Analyze it.* Take a paragraph of your story and, on another piece of paper, make a dash for each word in each sentence. It will look something like this:

   1. – – –. 2. – – – – – – – – –. 3.– – – – – –.
   4. – – – – – – – – – – – – – – – –. 5.– – –.

   Do you write long sentences or short ones? Never mind. Do you write sentences that are all the same length? This can be boring for the reader. Analyzing sentence length will remind you to vary the length of your sentences, making some long, some medium, and a few short and punchy. That will help give your stories a nice sense of pace.

6. *Punch it up.* As you read your story over, try to see

where it needs a little dash of suspense, some good description, a realistic smattering of dialogue, a touch of the hero's inner feelings, a haunting dream, the words of a song someone is singing, a mysterious note inserted into your narrative. Punch your writing up. Put it in orbit.

7. *Cut it down.* Did you overdo your description of Mr. Rabbit's garden? How many cabbages, after all, must you describe before we get the idea? Or do you have long strings of adjectives knotted together like tails on kites? Are you overwriting, overdescribing, overly long in every way? Cut. Clip. Chop. Keep it moving. Keep it brisk. Keep it unencumbered. Make sure that every word that's there belongs and that every word that belongs is there.

8. *Copy it over.* When you have made sure that your writing is the best writing you are capable of at the moment, copy it over neatly and send it on its way.

Meet the Author—
It's Me!

It ain't over till it's over.

YOGI BERRA

Carol Lea Benjamin always wanted to be a writer. After graduating from college, she worked as a detective, an editor, an English teacher whose strongest interest was teaching writing, and then a dog trainer. Her first book was called *Dog Training for Kids*, and since then she has written many books for children and adults, including *Running Basics, Dog Tricks, Dog Problems, Cartooning for Kids, Mother Knows Best: The Natural Way to Train Your Dog*, and two novels, *The Wicked Stepdog* and *Nobody's Baby Now*.

Ms. Benjamin lives in New York City, and Gardiner, New York, with her husband, architect Stephen Lennard, and their dog, Scarlet.

Photo: Stephen Lennard

THE QUOTATIONS THAT APPEAR IN THIS BOOK ARE FROM THE FOLLOWING SOURCES:

CHAPTER 2 WRITING FOR KIDS p. 7: Tina Mummery, *15 Magazine*, the publication of the Fifteenth Street School. (All quotes from *15 Magazine* appeared in 1970 and 1971.) p. 8: Maria Beatty, *15 Magazine*. pp. 8–9: Jay Rubinstein, *15 Magazine*. p. 9: Judy Blume, *Are You There God? It's Me, Margaret*. New York: Yearling Books/Dell 1970 (paper). pp. 9–10: Gerald Durrell, *My Family and Other Animals*. New York: Penguin Books, 1959, 1977. pp. 10–11: Kathy Weinert, *15 Magazine*. p. 11: Joy Adamson, *Born Free: A Lioness of Two Worlds*. New York: Vintage Books/Random House, 1960, 1974. p. 12: Michele Bean, *15 Magazine*. p. 12: Roger Tory Peterson, *How to Know the Birds*. New York: Signet Books/NAL, 1949, 1957 (paper). p. 13: Celia Converse, *15 Magazine*. p. 13: William Zinsser, *On Writing Well*. New York: Harper & Row, 1980 (paper). CHAPTER 7 AH! INSPIRATION! p. 38: Rebecca Lobl, *15 Magazine*. p. 40: Russell Baker, *Growing Up*. New York: Congdon & Weed, 1982. pp. 40–41: Lynn Offerman, *15 Magazine*. p. 43: Paul Zindel, *Confessions of a Teenage Baboon*. New York: Bantam, 1977 (paper). p. 43: M. E. Kerr, *I'll Love You When You're More Like Me*. New York: Laurel Leaf/Dell, 1977 (paper). p. 44: James Joyce, *A Portrait of the Artist As a Young Man*. New York: Modern Library, 1916, 1944. pp. 45–46: Jack Finney, *Time and Again*. New York: Simon & Schuster, 1970 (paper). p. 46: Bram Stoker, *Dracula*. London: Sphere Books, 1912 (paper). pp. 46–47: Michael Krieg, *15 Magazine*. p. 48: Andy Weiss, *15 Magazine*. p. 50: Kathy Weinert, *15 Magazine*. pp. 50–51: Richard Adams, *Watership Down*. New York: Avon, 1972 (paper). p. 52: Robbie Dewey, *15 Magazine*. p. 53: Betsy Ehrenfeld, *15 Magazine*. p. 54: E. B. White, *Stuart Little*. New York: Harper & Row, 1945 (paper). p. 55: Betsy Ehrenfeld, *15 Magazine*. p. 55: Bruce Harold Wolk, "Tracking Down a Rare Breed," in *The American Kennel Gazette*, March 1982. p. 56: Ann Seranne, *The Joy of Giving Homemade Food*. New York: David McKay, 1978. p. 59: Betsy Ehrenfeld, *15 Magazine*. p. 59: Celia Converse, *15 Magazine*. p. 60: Sarah Thomas, *15 Magazine*. p. 61: Hester Mundis, *No He's Not a Monkey, He's an Ape and He's my Son*. New York: Crown, 1976. p. 68: Celia Converse, *15 Magazine*. CHAPTER 10 SENTENCE TO PARAGRAPH TO FINISHED PIECE p. 78: Martin Cruz Smith, *Gorky Park*. New York, Random House, 1981. p. 79: Isak Dinesen, *Out of Africa*. New York: Vintage Books/Random House, 1937 (paper). p. 79: William Steig, *The Bad Island*. New York: Windmill Books/Simon & Schuster, 1969. p. 79: James Thurber, "The Departure of Emma Inch," in *Thurber's Dogs*. New York: Simon & Schuster, 1955, 1983. p. 79: Lewis Thomas, *The Lives of a Cell*. New York: Viking, 1974. p. 79: Frank Conroy, *Stop-Time*. New York: Penguin Books, 1965. p. 80: Leo Tolstoy, *Anna Karenina*. London: William Heinemann, 1901. p. 80: Henry Roth, *Call It Sleep*. New York: Avon Books, 1934 (paper). p. 80: J. D. Salinger, *The Catcher in the Rye*. New York: Bantam, 1964 (paper). p. 80: Norman Mailer, *The Naked and the Dead*. New York: NAL, 1948 (paper). p. 81: Harry Mazer, *The Dollar Man*. New York: Laurel Leaf/Dell, 1974 (paper). p. 81: Robertson Davies, *Fifth Business*. New York: Penguin Books, 1970 (paper). p. 81: Isaac Bashevis Singer, *Lost in America*. Garden City, NY: Doubleday, 1981. p. 81: Jean de Brunhoff, *The Travels of Babar*. New York: Random House, 1934. p. 81: J.R.R. Tolkien, *The Hobbit*. Boston: Houghton Mifflin, 1966. CHAPTER 11 PRIVATE WRITING: KEEPING A JOURNAL pp. 90–91: T. J. Siegal, diary, in *The Ramapo Times*, publication of Camp Ramapo, August 1983. pp. 92–93: Anne Frank, *The Diary of a Young Girl*. New York: Pocket Books/Simon & Schuster, 1952 (paper).

Index

Adams, Richard, *Watership Down*, 50–51
Adamson, Joy, *Born Free*, 11
animals, 67
    pets, 47–51
    wild, 57–59
assignments, pretitled, 17–23, 26, 69–72

Baker, Russell, *Growing Up*, 40
Bean, Michele, "Pine Tree," 12
Beatty, Maria, "Janis," 8
beginning, middle, end, 18, 78–84
Blume, Judy, *Are You There God? It's Me, Margaret.*, 9
books, making, 24–32
    huge, 30–32
    small, 24–29
de Brunhoff, Jean, *The Travels of Babar*, 81
Carroll, Lewis, *Through the Looking Glass*, 73
communication, 7–8, 11–13
Conroy, Frank, *Stop-Time*, 79
Converse, Celia, "An Elephant," 59
    "Fred," 13
    "Pigeon," 68

Davies, Robertson, *Fifth Business*, 81
Dewey, Robbie, "A Good Idea," 52
diary, notebook, journal, 33–34, 67, 68, 76
    as daily habit, 87–88
    description of, 33, 89

as private exercise, 88–89
as tool, 87–88, 89
topics in, 90
Dinesen, Isak, *Out of Africa*, 79
dictionaries, 74–75, 76–77
    how to use, 75
dreams, 37–38, 67
Durrell, Gerald, *My Family and Other Animals*, 9–10

Ehrenfeld, Betsy, "An Appaloosa," 55
    "A brook is an unharnessed thing," 59
    "Ralph," 53
essay construction, 84
    See also reality, research.
Eve, 7

fantasy, 44–45, 70
finishing touches, 86, 94–97
Finney, Jack, *Time and Again*, 46
Frank, Anne, *The Diary of a Young Girl*, 92–93

Halboth, Victoria, "Any human can feel he's alone," 39
hobbies, writing about, 54–56, 69–70, 71

ideas, sources for, 35–68

journal. *See* diary.

Joyce, James, *A Portrait of the Artist As a Young Man*, 44

Kahn, Carol, "I Am a Little Girl," 10
  "Refugee of the Rain," 62–64
Kerr, M. E., *I'll Love You When You're More Like Me*, 43
Krieg, Michael, "There was a count," 46–47

leading questions, 34
Lennard, Jennifer, "I wish that I was home," 92
  "Mienne My Hamster," 49
Lobl, Rebecca, "The Devil," 38

Mailer, Norman, *The Naked and the Dead*, 80
Mazer, Harry, *The Dollar Man*, 81
Mummery, Tina, "Ice Cream," 7
Mundis, Hester, *No He's Not a Monkey, He's an Ape and He's My Son*, 61

nature, writing about, 57–59, 67
notions, weird, 51–52
notebook, writer's. *See* diary.

Offerman, Lynn, "An Old Man Thinking About What He Hates," 40–41
onomatopoeia, 75

Peterson, Roger Tory, *How to Know the Birds*, 12
pets, writing about, 47–51
photographs as inspiration, 61–67, 68

reality, 38–43, 70, 85
  doctored, 41–42, 70
research, 57–58, 86
Roth, Henry, *Call It Sleep*, 80
Rubinstein, Jay, "Growing Up," 8–9

Salinger, J. D., *The Catcher in the Rye*, 80
self, writing about, 1–6, 38
  writing for, 8–10, 13, 87-90
  See also diary.
sentences, 16, 26, 96
  half-finished, 17–19
  illustrated, 19–23
  opening, 78–83
Seranne, Anne, *The Joy of Giving Homemade Food*, 56
Siegal, T. J., "I Really Did It," 90–91
Singer, Isaac Bashevis, *Lost in America*, 81
Smith, Martin Cruz, *Gorky Park*, 78
Steig, William, *The Bad Island*, 79
Stoker, Bram, *Dracula*, 46
story construction, 82–86

Thomas, Lewis, *The Lives of a Cell*, 79
Thomas, Sarah, "City and Country," 60
Thurber, James, "The Departure of Emma Inch," 79
Tolkien, J.R.R., *The Hobbit*, 81
Tolstoy, Leo, *Anna Karenina*, 80
tricks of the trade, 94–97
Twain, Mark, "The difference between," 75

visualizing, 95–96

Weinert, Kathy, "Bosco," 50
  "Once I shota," 10–11
Weiss, Andy, "The Gerbils," 48
White, E. B., *Stuart Little*, 54
Wolk, Bruce Harold, "Tracking Down a Rare Breed," 55
words, 73-77

Zindel, Paul, *Confessions of a Teenage Baboon*, 43
Zinsser, William, *On Writing Well*, 13